Delightful DELHI A to Z

GEETIKA JAIN
& ARJUN JAIN

Lustre Press
Roli Books

AUTHOR'S NOTE OF THANKS

Thanks to Maya Sama,
Seema Ram, Anu Shastri
and Naveena Jaffa
for their advice and editing.

ISBN: 978-81-7436-899-7

Published by Roli Books, 2013
M-75, Greater Kailash-II Market
New Delhi-110 048, India
Tel. +91-11-4068 2000
Fax: ++91-11-2921 7185
Email. info@rolibooks.com
Website: www.rolibooks.com

Art Director: Bonita Vaz
Design: Clotilde Francillon
Production: Shaji Sahadevan

Printed and bound in India

CONTENTS

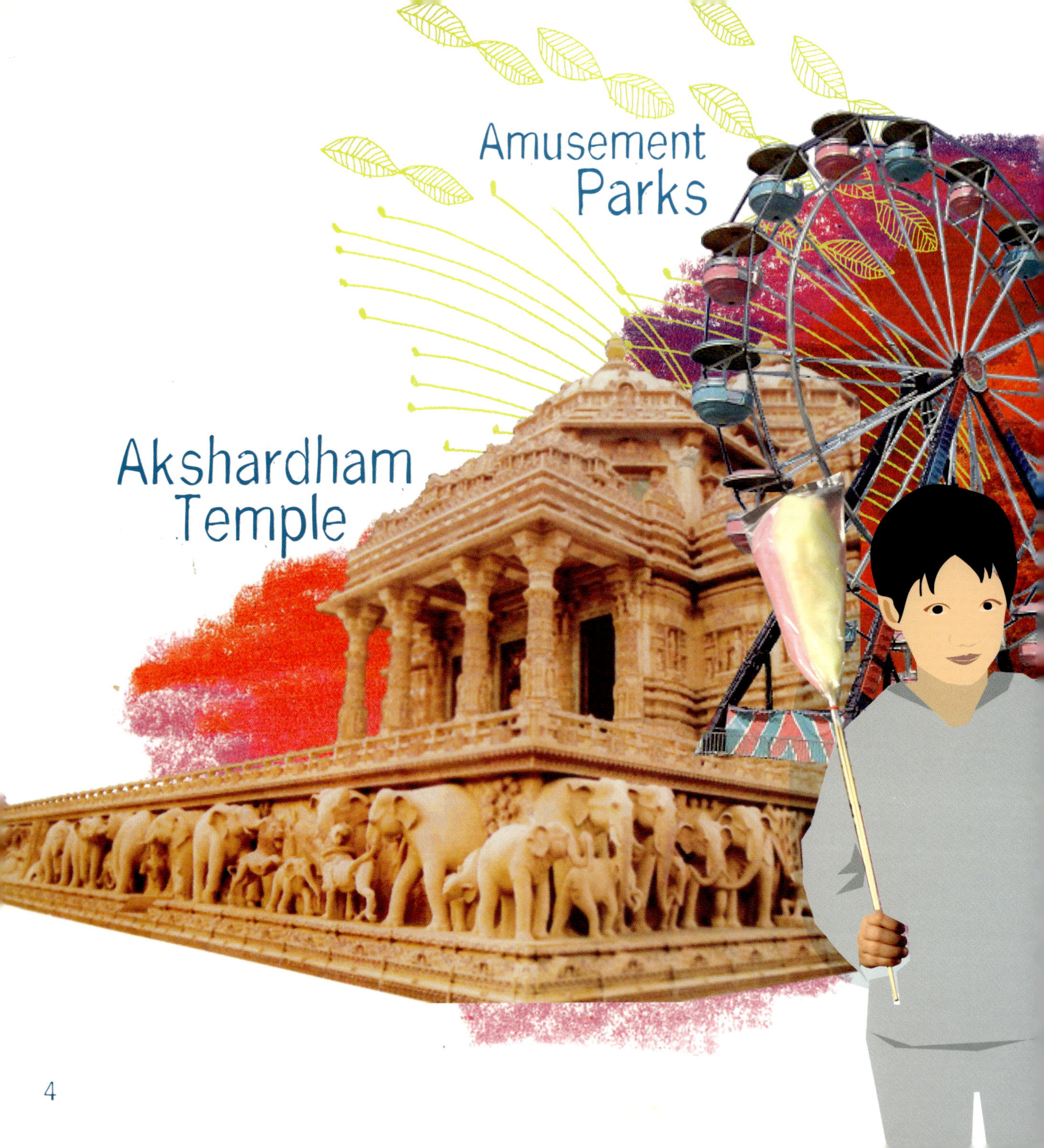
Amusement Parks
Akshardham Temple

A *a*

Air Force Museum

Auto Rickshaws

Bangles

Boating
at India Gate

Bus

Bb

Bal Bhavan

Balloon wala

Chandni
Chowk
Chai
wala
Cottage
Emporium

Cc

Lifestyle crafts for urban India
Dhaba
Dilli Haat

Dd
Deer Park
Dolls Museum
GO
Muthoot Group
Delhi Daredevils

Elephants on the road

Eating out

E *e*

Feroz
Shah Kotla
Cricket stadium
Football
Feral
dogs
Flowers

Ff

Fortune tellers

Gurudwara
Bangla Sahib
Gandhi
Smriti

Gg
Gas
Cylinder Delivery
Garden
of five senses

Horse riding
Hawker
Hanuman
Mandir Mela

Hh

Humayun's tomb

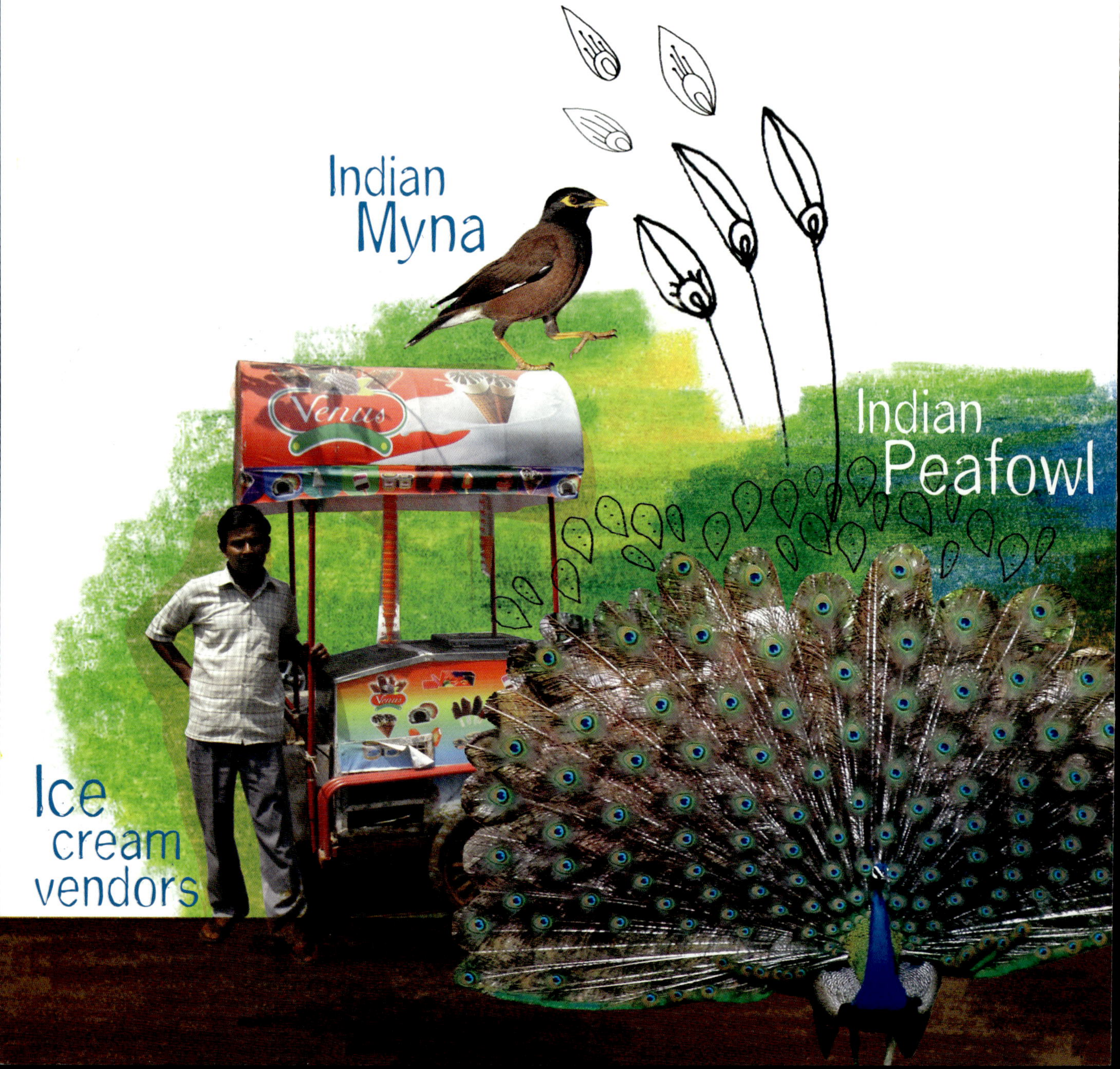
Indian Myna
Indian Peafowl
Venus
Ice cream vendors

Ii

India Gate

Juice Stalls
Mix FRUIT JUICE
Mix FRUIT JUICE
चौधरी जूस कार्नर
फ्रूट जूस
ताज़े फलों का रस
फ्रूट जूस
सच्चाई सफाई पवित्रता
FRESH JUICE
ORANGE JUICE VANILLA SHAKE BANANA SHAKE
Fruit Juice
Mango Shake
Fresh Fruit Juice
Jharu walis
Jantar Mantar

J

Jama Masjid

Kikar tree
Khan Market
Kingdom of Dreams
Keys held by Parking assistants
Café Turtle
FULL CIRCLE
NEEMRANA

Kite flying

Lodhi
Gardens

Lutyens'
Delhi

Ll

Mehndi

Metro

M m
Malls
THE GALAXY
Half Marathon
Airtel
Delhi Half Marathon
Airtel Delhi
Marathon
Monkey dance

National
Science Centre
Natural
History Museum
NEHRU
and Memorial
Planetarium

Nn
National Gallery of Modern Art

Old fort
Over loaded vehicles
EICHER

Old Delhi

Press wali

Polo

Paan Wala

Police

P p

Puppeteers

Qq
Qutab Minar
Qawwali

Red Fort
Rashtrapati Bhavan
Republic Day Parade

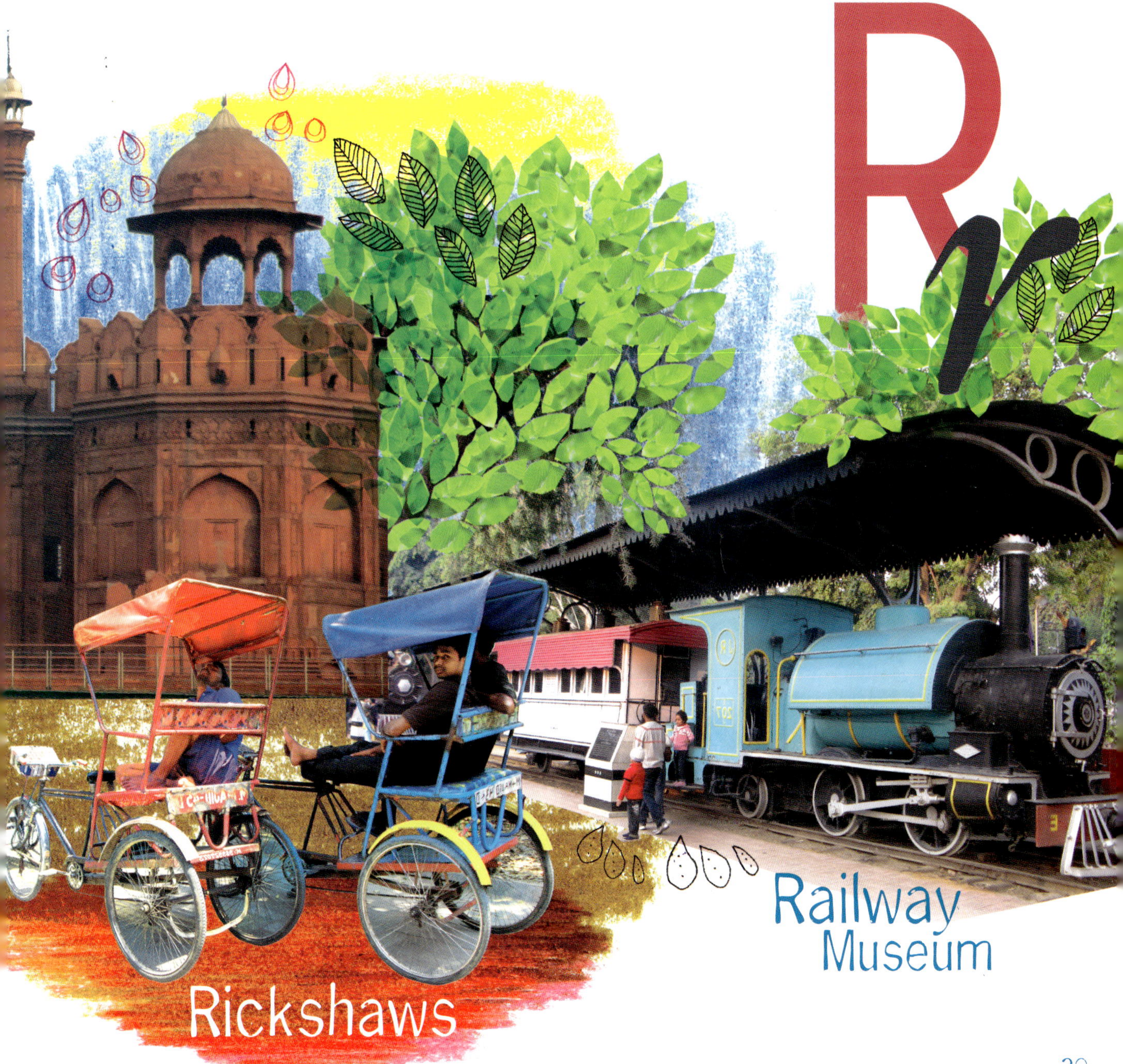

Railway Museum

Rickshaws

Slums

Snake charmer

Sound and light SHOW
S s
gurjari
State Emporia
Shaadi

Truck

Tt
Toys
Tandoor
Taxi

Urinators in the streets

Uniforms

Ugrasen ki Baoli

Vendors

Vintage Car Rally

Words
on vehicles

Warding
off the evil eye

W w
Water cart
Wildlife

X-citing festivals

Christmas

X x
Dussehra
Ph.: 23276311, 23267834
Diwali
Eid
Rakhee

Yamuna
river

Yy

Zoo

Z z

Delightful Delhi

a book for children and for curious minds of all ages

An A-Z of things you'll see in Delhi

AIR FORCE MUSEUM

This museum at Palam Air Force Station showcases the history of the Indian Air Force. From the initial days of World War 1, when Indian aviators flew for the Royal Flying Corps, to the recent Operation Kargil. The photographs, badges and uniforms make captivating displays. An enormous hangar holds aircrafts including the Spitfire, Gnat, Hawker Hunter, MiG-21 and Sukhoi-7 and a troop and freight carrier. On October 8th, Air-force Day is celebrated with additional aircrafts on view as well as an impressive Indian Air Force parade. *Location: Palam Road, Delhi Cantonment, Tel. 011 2569 7551*

AKSHARDHAM TEMPLE

Built over a hundred acres on the banks of the Yamuna, this impressive Hindu Temple complex is dedicated to Bhagwan Swaminarayan. The temple showcases the 18th century sage's spiritual journey and teachings. India's history, art, culture and values are also depicted via an animatronics show, a boat ride and a large screen film. There are other features worth exploring such as the musical fountains and lotus gardens. *Location: NH24, Noida Mor, Tel. 011 2201 6688 or 2202 6688*

AMUSEMENT PARKS

- Aapno Ghar-43rd Mile Stone Village, Shikhopur on NH-8, the Delhi-Jaipur Highway, Tel. 0124 237 2251

- Adventure Island, Metro Walk, Sector 10, Rohini, opposite Rithala Metro Station, Tel. 011 4704 1111

- Worlds of Wonder@Entertainment City, The Great India Place, Plot No. A2, Sector 38, Noida, Tel. 0120 465 0000

- Fun and Food Village, Gurgaon road, Kapashera Estate, New Delhi, Tel. 011 4326 0000

AUTO RICKSHAW

Also known as a 'three-wheeler', this noisy, light vehicle is usually hired to cover short distances and carries up to three passengers. Many auto rickshaws are lovingly decorated with images of movie stars on the seat covers and painted phrases on the rear. The government-enforced switch from petrol to CNG gas has helped improve the air quality in Delhi.

Bb

BAL BHAVAN

The Bal Bhavan National Children's Museum and Aquarium is a museum as well as an interactive space with workshops. The 'Hamara Bharat' permanent gallery displays Indian cultural heritage and achievements in science and technology. Children can see collections of toys and currency from around the world, ride a train, explore an aviary and aquarium and take part in art, drama, puppet-making, dance and music workshops. *Location: Kotla Road, near ITO, Tel. 011 2323 2672 or 2323 7856*

BALLOON WALA

An exciting sound for children everywhere in Delhi is the familiar tooting of the balloon walas before they come into sight. Laden with colourful balloons and cheap plastic toys such as kitchen-sets, dolls, watches, cameras and catapults, they walk or cycle through neighbourhoods or base themselves in markets and park corners where children can easily find them.

BANGLES

Traditionally worn to signify a woman's married status, bangles are very popular and are enjoyed by girls and women all over India. They are made of a vast array of materials such as glass, silver, gold, diamonds and lac (lacquer studded with decorative mirror pieces). Sikh and Hindu brides typically wear a set of red and white bangles called *choora* on both wrists for forty days. *Bangles can be bought in markets such as Lajpat Nagar's Central Market, Dilli Haat and Hanuman Mandir mela (fair) on Tuesdays.*

BOATING AT INDIA GATE

Boating at India Gate is a popular activity with the locals who also like to picnic on the adjoining lawns. Dozens of ice-cream vans, balloon walas and toy vendors line-up on the gravel edges of Rajpath. In the evenings, it is a beautiful sight when the fountains are lit up in many vibrant colours.

BUS

Buses take care of over 60% of Delhi's transport needs. Each day over 8,000 buses traverse the roads of Delhi, and the DTC (Delhi Transport Corporation) has the world's largest fleet of CNG-powered buses.

Cc

CHAI WALA

Chai walas and their tea stalls can be seen absolutely everywhere, from large markets to the tiniest alleyways. The thick brown mix of water, tea leaves, milk and spices simmering in a pot is well-loved by Dilli walas. A dash of sugar and the moment is elevated. The serving of the tea sometimes becomes a performance when a long, thin, stream of tea, poured from afar fills rows of glasses without spilling a drop.Ustad Chai Wala in Old Delhi near Jama Masjid serves tea with cream and has a huge following.

CHANDNI CHOWK

Although crowded and bustling, a rickshaw ride through the historic neighbourhood of Chandni Chowk can be an interesting adventure for curious children. The street itself was once the central avenue and the royal processional route of Shahjahanabad, the city of Emperor Shah Jahan. Kinari bazaar with its enthralling bridal accessories, Dariba Kalan's jewellery shops, Khari Baoli spice market and the food stalls around Parathe Wali Gali are particularly worth visiting. It is a good idea to get a guide from the nearby Red Fort who can show you the highlights and share interesting anecdotes.

COTTAGE EMPORIUM

This large Government-run enterprise sells traditional handicrafts from various states in India. It is a great place to see what artisans are making in the far corners of the country. The children's area has some wonderful books, toys and gifts. *Location: Jawahar Vyapar Bhavan on Janpath, Tel. 011 2332 0439 www.cottageemporium.in*

COW

The cow is humorously referred to as a 'brake inspector' by drivers who come to an abrupt halt as a cow casually steps on the road. Considered sacred by the Hindus, cow slaughter is banned in most of India and thousands of cows wander around freely, eating what they find. In 2002, the residents of Delhi signed a petition to have them removed and the City has employed 'cow-catchers' who round them up and take them to cow sanctuaries funded by Hindu charities and the government. Even now, there are a few thousand stray cows living on the streets of Delhi.

CRAFTS MUSEUM

This pleasant museum with a sprawling, tree-shaded outdoor area is a wonderful place to see India's traditional arts and crafts. Watch artisans make Madhubani paintings, carve toys from tree pith and create animals of clay. You might even catch a puppet show or a dance. The indoor museum showcases metal, woodwork and textile collections. The souvenir shop has an exceptionally good selection and you can also make purchases directly from the artisans. *Location: Gate no. 2 Bhairon Road, Pragati Maidan, Tel. 011 2337 1887*

DEER PARK

One of Delhi's most loved and child-friendly parks, Deer Park can be accessed from Hauz Khas Village and Safdarjung Enclave. There are several picnic spots and walks along a lake surrounded by trees that are filled with birds. Children can feed the spotted-deer, guinea pigs, rabbits and peacocks. Nehru Park, Sanjay Van and Buddha-Jayanti Park are also wonderful spots for outings with children.

DELHI DAREDEVILS

Delhi Daredevils is one of twelve IPL (Indian Premier League) sponsored Twenty20 cricket teams. Home matches are played on Feroz Shah Kotla grounds and the IPL matches run from April to June. Virendra Sehwag is one of the team's iconic players. The Daredevils' logo is a zooming cricket ball on fire, their colours are navy blue and red and the team anthem is 'Khel front foot par' (play aggressively). *The team can be followed on Facebook and Twitter, their website is www.delhidaredevils.com*

DHABA

Dhabas are open-air restaurants, usually dotted along major highways, catering to truck drivers. They are also found in cities, and there are many in Delhi. The typically casual kitchens with a few tables and chairs serve Punjabi cuisine such as dal makhni, butter chicken, palak paneer and tandoori rotis. They are very popular as the food is fresh, delicious and affordable. *Some of the favorites: Rajinder Dhaba at Safdarjung Enclave, Shiv Dhaba at Kalkaji, Ganga Dhaba at JNU and Nand Lal Dhaba at Darya Ganj.*

DILLI HAAT

Dilli Haat is a lively, outdoor marketplace modelled after a village haat or market where many wonderful crafts such as wooden and papier maché toys, puppets, bangles, paper crafts, furniture and textiles are showcased. The salespeople are usually the artisans themselves and they can explain exactly how the items were crafted. The stalls keep changing, so if you visit after a while, you will come across new crafts. See a magic show or a dance performance and enjoy food from many parts of India. *Location: Opposite INA Market Tel. 011 2611 9055 OR Pitampura Tel. 011 2731 7663*

DOLLS MUSEUM

The Shankar's International Dolls Museum has over five thousand dolls from all over the world, including dolls from the different states of India in local costume. The collection was founded in 1957 by cartoonist K. Shankar Pillai who brought back dolls from his travels. Over the years, many visiting dignitaries gifted dolls from their countries. *Location: Nehru House, Bahadur Shah Zafar Marg*

EATING-OUT

One of Delhi's greatest delights is the variety of delicious food one can find in the streets, market kiosks and restaurants. Gol gappa, dahi papri and aloo-tikki are some of the savoury snacks called Chaat. Tandoori chicken, paneer tikka, daal makhni are dishes from the popular 'Mughlai' cuisine while gulab jamun, gajar ka halwa, rasmalai and kulfi are the much loved sweets. Look out for seasonal fruits such as mango, phalsa and jamun.

ELEPHANTS ON THE ROAD

Elephants have been a vital part of India's cultural history for over three thousand years and the art of domestication originated in the North East. For centuries elephants have been used for logging, religious processions, active combat in wartime and in the circus. Even today they transport supplies and soldiers to areas where trucks cannot go. Due to bans on logging, domesticated elephants are now used in forest reserves and for tourism. Mahouts are the trainers and carers of elephants. It is not unusual to come across a mahout sitting atop an elephant walking on the streets of Delhi. People, especially children, like to make contact with the animal, give it a piece of fruit or even a tip to the mahout.

F *f*

FERAL DOGS

On recent count, officials reported that there were about 250,000 feral or stray dogs living on the streets of Delhi. They are found everywhere, in neighbourhoods, in markets and even on the major roads. There is talk of reducing their count by sterilisation. Many people feed them and even give them coats in the winter. It is best not to touch or play with a stray dog.

FIROZ SHAH KOTLA CRICKET STADIUM

Dilliwalas, like other Indians, are crazy about cricket and the sport is played in the grounds, gardens and narrow alleys of Delhi. Test Matches can be viewed at the stadium affectionately known as 'The Kotla' on Bahadur Shah Zafar Marg from September to March. *The IPL Twenty20 matches are on from April to June, Tel. 011 2331 9323*

FLOWERS

All over Delhi, beautiful cut flowers are available on roadside stalls found in colonies and markets. The wholesale flower markets have recently been relocated to a central location in Ghazipur with cold storage facilities. A stunning array of roses, gladioli, marigolds, orchids, chrysanthemums, tube-roses and daisies are sold in bunches, by weight or by the inch in garlands. Children enjoy bringing home baskets of flowers to arrange on the floor, rangoli-style or to design their own floral jewellery.

FOOTBALL

Football matches and neighbourhood games played by boys' and mens' teams are becoming a regular sight in Delhi. The sport is particularly popular at some of Delhi's elite schools. The Delhi International Football League (DIFL) holds matches at the Ambedkar Stadium. *www.difl.org*

FORTUNE TELLERS

The tradition of fortune telling is an old one; many Indians like to visit palmists, tarot card readers and numerologists. Fortune telling parrots and cows can be seen in tourist-spots, fairs and haats. When asked, 'Who will be successful?' the colourfully decked cow will spin around and face an audience-member. Parrots pop out of their cages, choose a card from a pile, the fortune is read out by the keeper and the parrot goes back into its cage. These tamashas are popular in rural India.

G g

GANDHI SMRITI AND MUSEUM

Dedicated to the Father of the Nation, Mahatma Gandhi, this museum is a wonderful place to learn about his life and message. Gandhiji's spartan room and belongings are just the way he left them on January 30th 1948, the day he was assassinated in the gardens of this house. In the museum upstairs are photographs and films through which one can get to know more about the great thinker and leader. *Location: Birla House, 5 Tees January Marg www.gandhismriti.gov.in*

GARDEN OF FIVE SENSES

Touch the rocks, smell the flowers, see the beautiful landscape, hear the waterfalls and taste the delicious food at the Garden of Five Senses, a sprawling, 20-acre space. It is a wonderful venue for picnics with children who can ride the solar powered cars and explore the sculpture gardens. *Location: Saiyad ul Ajaib village, near Saket*

GAS CYLINDER DELIVERY

The sight of LPG (Liquid Petroleum Gas) or cooking-gas cylinders being delivered to various homes is not uncommon. On the streets of Delhi, one can see tempos, carts, rickshaws and bicycles carting and delivering the red cylinders all over, especially in winter, when the demand goes up. Once they reach their destination, the heavy 20 kilo cylinders are rolled on the ground towards the kitchen. Even though gas is piped to some colonies, the gas cylinder is the mainstay of most Delhi kitchens.

GURUDWARA BANGLA SAHIB

The white marble temple with its beautiful gold plated dome is where the Sikhs go for spiritual reflection, to listen to devotional singing and to serve others. The Gurudwara is dedicated to Guru Harkrishan Dev ji. The Sunday morning langar, a free community-kitchen meal is very popular. *Location: Ashok Road, near Connaught Place*

H h

HANUMAN MANDIR MELA

On Tuesdays, Hanuman Mandir sees a larger than ever stream of devotees at the temple. Hanuman is deemed to have appeared here in his childhood avatar, known as Bala Hanuman. The popular fair teems with mehndiwalis (henna tattoo artists), bangle sellers and astrologers. *Location: Baba Kharak Singh Marg, near Rajiv Chowk*

HAWKER

Hawkers are people who sell their wares on the go. They sometimes carry a stand on which they display their goods. In Delhi you can see hawkers selling things like sprouted lentils, roasted corn, boiled sweet-potatoes, toys, sun-glasses and flowers. The Delhi Hawkers Welfare Association, or the Reri Patri Sangharsh Morcha, attempts to restrict large corporations entering the retail space for fear that it would affect the livelihoods of around 600,000 hawkers in the city.

HORSE RIDING

- The Delhi Horse Show is a spectacular event held in February or March, competitors from all over India can be seen show-jumping, tent pegging and performing dressage. *Location: B Squadron 61 Cavalry, Cariappa Marg, Delhi Cantonment. Tel. 011 2569 9444 or 2569 9666*

- The army Polo and Riding club offers spectacular Polo Tournaments in October, November and February. *Location: Cariappa Marg, Cantonment.*

- Children can practice and enjoy horse riding at the following places:

- DDA Saket Sports Complex, J Block Saket 011 2956 1742.
- Beeya's Riding Facility offers ponies as well as horses, making it a great place for beginners. Munirka Farms, off Green Avanue in Vasant Kunj Tel: 98 100 62736
-The Children's Riding Club offers lessons for children aged four and above in the afternoons. Location: Safdarjung road, Safdarjung Enclave. www.childrensridingclub.com Tel. 98 106 79090 Or Race Course Road, Tel. 011 2301 2265

HUMAYUN'S TOMB

Humayun's tomb is one of the earliest and best examples of Mughal architecture in Delhi. Along with Qutab Minar and the Red Fort, it has the status of a UNESCO World Heritage Site. The edifice was started around 1566 for Humayun by his wife, Hamida Banu Begum and even today the beautiful buildings, fountain-laden gardens and water channels are enjoyed by visitors. *Location: on Mathura Road, near the crossing with Lodhi Road*

ICE CREAM VENDORS

Ice cream vendors are found all over Delhi, a welcome sight for adults and children alike. Orange bar, chocobar, mango duet and the ice-cream filled cones are most popular. A particularly interesting outing for children is to Nirula's Ice-cream Museum. Here, they learn about the history of ice cream, how it is made and plenty of related trivia. *The museum is open twice a week for children of ages 7-11 by appointment only. Location: C-135 Sector 2, Noida. Tel. 95 120 244 52607*

INDIA GATE

This iconic sandstone arch was designed by Sir Edwin Lutyens in 1921. At first a memorial to the British Indian Army soldiers who lost their lives during World War I, it is now the Indian Army's Tomb of the Unknown Soldier. A permanent flame, known as the 'Amar Javan Jyoti' honours them. There is a beautiful view of Rashtrapati Bhavan from one side of the arch.

INDIAN MYNA

The Myna, a brown bird with yellow legs, beak and eyes, can easily be spotted all over Delhi as it lives close to human habitation, often foraging in rubbish heaps and sneaking into houses for titbits. In folklore, songs and poetry, the parakeet (tota) and myna, are often paired. Schoolgirls count their numbers to make predictions; 'One for sorrow, two for joy, three for a letter, four for a toy. Five for silver, six for gold, seven for a secret never to be told.'

INDIAN PEAFOWL

The familiar mayon-mayon calls often reveal our spectacular National Bird, the 'Peacock' (commonly known after the male of the species). Peafowl can be sighted in the Ridge Forest, Buddha Jayanti Park, Deer Park and even in residential neighbourhoods where greenery is abundant. The male has an iridescent blue neck and breast, a crest and a long trail of feathers. This is raised and opened to form a fan-like shape, revealing colourful spots. During courtship, peacocks quiver their open feathers in a magnificent display to attract females. Peahens have duller plumage and much shorter tail feathers. Children like to collect peacock feathers and keep them in their books for good luck.

JAMA MASJID

Jama Masjid or 'Friday Mosque', is named after the holy day of the Muslims. Built by Mughal Emperor Shah Jahan in 1656, this exquisite mosque made of red sandstone and white marble is India's largest, with the ability to hold up to 25,000 worshippers in its compound. The streets around it are filled with bazaars and food kiosks. The southern minaret has wonderful views of Old and New Delhi.

JANTAR MANTAR

Built in the early 1700s by the Maharaja of Jaipur, this pink sandstone observatory was made to track the movement of the sun and the stars. Children enjoy learning about its functions, climbing its curious structures, discovering the nooks and crannies and running around in the gardens. *Location: Parliament Street, close to Rajeev Chowk*

JHARU WALIS

Each morning, the streets of the city come alive with several thousand women in their traditional, colourful salwaar-kameez and dupatta. They sweep away dust and rubbish with their long brooms called jharus. These safai karamcharis or cleanliness workers are either regular employees of the MCD (Municipal Corporation of Delhi) earning from ₹ 2,000 to 4,000 a month or day-wagers who make ₹ 130 per day.

JUICE STALL

Freshly squeezed juice is a readily available delight from Delhi's many juice stalls. Oranges, mangoes, pomegranates, carrots and papayas are piled high and a glassful of delicious juice with or without masala is handed out to quench one's thirst. The banners of the juice stalls tend to be very colourful with the hallmark hand painted signs in faceted font and images of movie stars. If you look at the banner carefully, you might even find the signature of the legendary artist Charan, of Charan Arts Studio in Top Sarai, near Chandini Chowk.

Kk

KEYS HELD BY PARKING ATTENDANTS

A rather inventive way of getting a lot of cars into a small parking lot is to have the parking attendant take your keys, park the car in neutral gear and roll it out for you again when you are ready to leave. Attendants cleverly pack many cars together, moving them around as and when needed by pushing them. They hold dozens of keys in a large metal loop. People often wonder how they match the right key and car.

KHAN MARKET

Favoured by Delhi's elite, Khan Market is packed with bookshops, restaurants and shops selling merchandise ranging from home products, fruits and groceries to jewellery, photography-equipment and fashion wear. Children like the toy stores, bookshops as well as the edible treats. After India's partition, this land was allocated to immigrants from the North-West Frontier Province of Pakistan and the market was named after Khan Abdul Ghaffar Khan, a Pashtun political and spiritual leader. Khan Market is the most valuable real estate in Delhi.

KIKAR TREE

Many species of trees can be seen in Delhi including Neem, Peepul, Laburnum, Gulmohar and Semul. The Kikar or Acacia tree grew in abundance before the British began large scale planting of other species. This thorn tree survives well in dry conditions and sprouts yellow blossoms in spring.

KINGDOM OF DREAMS

This vast entertainment complex in Gurgaon showcases song and dance performances, movies and food from India's different states. *Contact&location: Great India Nautanki Company Ltd. Auditorium complex, Sector 29, Gurgaon 122001, Haryana, Tel. 91 0124 452 8000*

KITE FLYING

Kite flying is an important part of Delhi's culture, and it peaks during the harvest festival of Makar Sankranti in January, and also in the lead up to August 15th, Independence Day, when the markets are filled with stalls selling kites, string and reel. Flying kites symbolises freedom and many kites bear India's tricolour. *An amazing array of kites can be bought at Jawahar Kite house and Bishan Chand and Sons in Lal Kuan Market in Old Delhi.*

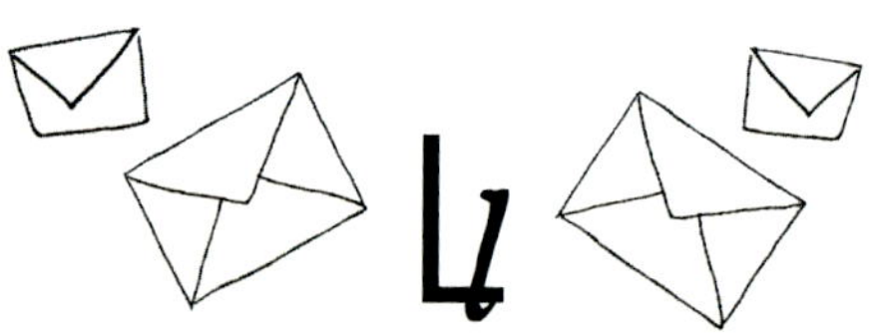

LABOURERS

Delhi is a city perpetually under construction, be it private homes, commercial or Goverment buildings. Skilled and unskilled labourers or masons who work on these projects earn daily wages under ₹ 250 per day. They live in slums or travel to Delhi from neighbouring states, bringing along their mid-day meal. Women often have to bring their small children to the construction site if there is no one to look after them at home.

LETTERBOX

The red cylinder-shaped letterbox with a rounded top is a familiar sight all over India. A new, rectangular shape is also visible in many places. The Indian Postal Service has over 155,000 post offices, making it the most extensive postal service in the world.

LODHI GARDENS

This tree-shaded oasis was laid out in 1936 by the British who relocated a village to create space for the garden. The gardens are a great favourite of Dilli walas. They are dotted with tombs of the Sayyid and Lodhi Sultans of the 16th century. It is a popular spot for a walk, a jog or a picnic. Explore the green house, the bonsai park and the eight-arched bridge. The Lodhi Garden restaurant near Gate 1 has a picturesque setting. *Location: Lodhi Road, near Safdarjung's tomb*

LOTUS TEMPLE

The Baha'i House of Worship is known as the Lotus Temple as it has been built in the shape of a lotus flower comprising 27 petals which appear to float on the gardens. Designed by Iranian architect Faribroz Sahba, it was built in 1986.

Location: Opposite Kalkaji Mandir, near Nehru place

LUTYENS DELHI

Lutyens Delhi is the area in New Delhi named after the British architect Sir Edwin Lutyens, who designed and built New Delhi over twenty years from 1912 to 1931, after Delhi was chosen to replace Calcutta as the seat of the British-Indian Government. He developed what he called the 'New Order of Classical Architecture' borrowing from traditional Indian styles of building; the dome of the Viceroy's house (now Rashtrapati Bhavan) is a drum-mounted Buddhist dome. There are pavilions (chattris), stone lattice screens and carved images of elephants. The material used is red sandstone as in the Mughal style buildings. Lutyens also designed India Gate and Hyderabad House. He earmarked the space for wide tree-lined avenues, parliament buildings and bungalows.

M m

MALLS

Dozens of fancy malls have come up in the NCR (National Capital Region). Children are spending increasing amounts of time in play areas, video arcades and entertainment zones in Malls. The air conditioned space is a huge attraction in the extreme heat of summer.

- Ambience Mall, NH-8, Gurgaon, there are a variety of gaming experiences on Level 4

- Ansal Plaza, Funkie Orbit play area, Andews Ganj

- Metropolitan Mall, MG Road, Gurgaon offers bowling, video games and a trampoline at Amoeba

- Select City Mall in Saket, Emporio Mall in Vasant Kunj and Spice World in Noida have wonderful play areas for younger children.

MARATHON

The Marathon in Delhi is a half-marathon, covering a distance of 21.097 km. It usually starts at the Nehru Stadium. The Great Delhi Run (7km), Senior Citizens Run (4.3km) and Wheelchair Run (2.5km) are also held around the same time. *If you wish to participate, contact Manzar Khan at Delhi Int'l Marathon Office, N126 Panchsheel Park, New Delhi for details, Tel. 91 98 9165 8183*

MEHNDI

Although Mehndi (henna) is usually put on occasions such as weddings and festivals, young girls enjoy stopping at stalls in markets and bazaars to have beautiful and intricate designs drawn onto their hands. Mehndi is the paste of a tropical plant mixed with oil and lemon. When it dries, it leaves behind a deep red colour which lasts for a couple of weeks. *Mehndi walis can be found in many places such as the markets, Dilli Haat and Janpath.*

METRO

The Metro is the subway-train network that serves the National Capital Region of Delhi and carries an average of 1.5 million commuters daily. Clean and efficient, it is a welcome addition to the transport of Delhi. There are 6 lines that extend over 161 kilometres. So far, there are well over 135 stations of which more than 31 are underground. The first carriage is reserved for ladies. *Visit the Metro Museum at Patel Chowk station.*

MONKEY DANCE

The sound of a dumroo or small drum in the neighbourhoods announces the arrival of the man with his monkeys. The rhesus monkeys are usually dressed as a bride and groom, and a humorous scene unfolds where she refuses to marry him at first, but eventually does after some cajoling. Shows such as these are a relic of the past as these animals should be left in the wild and not captured and trained for our entertainment.

There was a time when the 'Bandar aur Madari ka Kartab', or the trainer-and monkey show could be seen all over Delhi. Monkey and bear dances have been banned under the Wildlife Protection Act, a positive step to prevent them from being taken from the wild for this purpose. Rhesus Macaques can often be a nuisance in some areas so langurs are brought in by their trainers to scare them off. Even the Government employs langurs for this purpose. The sight of a man on a bicycle with a langur is now more common than the dancing monkeys.

NATIONAL GALLERY OF MODERN ART

This impressive gallery showcases the works of India's greatest artists from the 1850s to present day in a beautiful Lutyens building. Explore paintings by Raja Ravi Varma, Amrita Shergill and the members of the Progressive Arts Movement. The outdoor sculpture gardens are worth exploring too. *Location: Jaipur House near India Gate. Tel. 011 2338 4560*

NATIONAL SCIENCE CENTRE

Pre-historic life, Fun Science, Human Biology and Emerging Technology are just some of the exciting galleries at this well equipped and thoroughly interesting science museum, a must for curious children of all ages. *Location: Bhairon Road, near Gate 1, Pragati Maidan. Tel. 011 2337 1893/1297*

NATURAL HISTORY MUSEUM

This museum is where one can learn about the flora and fauna of India through films and dioramas of animals in their natural habitat. There is an exhibit about the eco systems of the world as well as one on dinosaurs. In need of renovation, this tired museum could become an outstanding venue for children. *Location: FICCI Building on Barakhamba Road by Mandi house*

NEHRU MEMORIAL MUSEUM AND PLANETARIUM

Known as Teen Murti Bhavan, this gracious residence with an enormous garden was built in 1930 for the British Commander in Chief of the Army. Jawaharlal Nehru stayed there after Independence and it is now a museum where you can wander through some of the rooms and offices that Nehru ji and his family occupied and get a sense of how they lived.

Budding astronomers will find lots to discover at the planetarium in the same complex. The sky theatre has an impressive dome-shaped screen made up of 26 curved parts where 40 minute shows such as 'Ultimate Universe' and 'Astronaut' are held. There are observation activities, changing exhibits as well as interactive models. A key attraction is the Soyuz T 10 which carried India's first cosmonaut Rakesh Sharma to space. *Location: Teen Murti House, Teen Murti Road. www.nehruplanetarium.org Tel. 011 2301 2994*

OLD DELHI

A walk or a rickshaw ride through this neighbourhood, with its crumbling courtyard houses and narrow, bustling streets, takes you back in time. Wholesale traders sell bridal clothing, jewellery, toys, electronics, spices and other wares. Eat at the legendary stalls of Parathe Wali Gali and try a specialty made with milk foam known as Daulat ki Chaat. The spice market at Khari Baoli is a vision with bagfuls of red chillies being traded. Look out for the Jain Svatambar Temple, a little known jewel. This place offers rich material for budding photographers.

OLD FORT (*PURANA QILA*)

This sprawling fort with high walls has a curious and interesting history. It was started at around 1533 by the Mughal Emperor, Humayun, then seized by Sher Shah who continued to build it and then recaptured by Humayun. It is said to stand on the site of the ancient city of Indraprastha founded by Pandavas who are mentioned in the epic Mahabharat. There is a sound and light show in the evenings which brings all of Delhi's captivating history to life. *Location: Mathura Road*

OVERLOADED VEHICLES

Overloading is a way of life in many parts of India including Delhi. On the roads one can see buses with people spilling out, trucks with impossibly high stacks of hay and vendors with their merchandise ready to spill. It is amusing to see just how much can be packed onto the vehicles.

PAAN WALA

Colourful kiosks selling paan are a Delhi staple. The triangle shaped treat of areca nut, lime paste, rose preserve and fennel seeds folded in a Betel leaf is popular with adults who chew it after dinner as a digestive or anytime in the day as a pick-me-up. Different versions of paan are enjoyed in a wide belt from Pakistan to Papua New Guinea.

POLICEMAN

The duty of Delhi Police is to prevent and investigate crime, protect women and control traffic. Their motto is 'Citizens First'. There are more than 80,000 personnel and approximately 136 stations across the NCR (National Capital Region).

The National Police Museum at the Central Bureau of Investigation HQ is worth a quick visit. Here, you can see seized articles, learn about police vigilance and how the latest forensic techniques are used to solve crimes. *Location: CGO Complex, Lodhi Road.*

POLO

Polo is known as 'the sport of kings.' It was brought to India by the British and was supported by the royal families. India is one of sixteen countries in the world that play professional polo. Delhi and Jaipur are the main centres where polo matches can be enjoyed. Visit the Jaipur Polo Grounds next to the Race Course and Gymkhana Club. Matches are played in the autumn season from October to mid-December and in spring from end-January to early March. Watching a match followed by tent pegging and other riding feats can be thoroughly enjoyable, as is the Mughlai food in the canteen.

PRESS WALI

You don't have to look far to spot a press wala in any residential neighbourhood in Delhi. A shaded corner under a tree or a nook beside a wall becomes his base. A makeshift plank forms a table and a smouldering pot of coals feeds the heavy, old fashioned iron that does not require electricity. Clothes for ironing are collected in the morning (usually by his helper) and for a few rupees each, they are professionally ironed and returned, folded or on hangers, by the evening. The pleasure of wearing a wrinkle-free sari or a well creased trouser is a gift of the local press wala, whose services are truly welcome.

PUPPETS

The art of kathputli or puppetry in India is older than the epics. Shadow, glove, rod and string puppet performances can be seen at various venues such as The Crafts Museum and Dilli Haat.

- At the Katkatha Puppets Arts Trust workshop, Habitat Arts centre, children can learn puppet making and have performances. *www.katkatha.org*

- At the House of Puppets, one can view dancing Rajasthani puppets and performances like fire-eating, stilt walking and magic shows on every second and fourth Saturday of the month.
Location: Kathputli Colony near Shadipur Depot, Tel. 91 99 683 84447

QAWWALI

A 750 year old form of devotional Sufi singing, qawwalis are songs sung by troupes of men accompanied with tablas, harmonium and rhythmic clapping. The songs are usually in Urdu and Punjabi and are intended to stir the listener into a spiritual trance. Singers are often invited to homes for performances.

- Join the Hope Project for a walk around the Dargah (shrine) in Nizamuddin. The walks end in qawwalis by Sufi singers on Thursday and Friday evenings.

QUTAB MINAR AND THE SURROUNDING COMPLEX

Qutab Minar was built as a victory tower to mark the arrival of Islam in this land. The 73 meter high, red sandstone and marble minaret was started in 1193 by Qutub-ud-din Aibak. At the base of the minaret is the beautiful Quwwat-ul-Islam Mosque and vast gardens with shade trees. In September, the colourful Phoolwaalon ki Sair (procession of the florists) originates in this area. In October, renowned musicians and singers perform at the Qutab Festival.

The area around Qutab Minar has many historic structures worth exploring such as Adam Khan's tomb, the stepwell known as Rajon ki Bain, Balban's Tomb, Jamali Kamali's tomb and Metcalf's Folly. The area got its name from the revered Sufi saint, Qutubuddin Bhaktiar Kaki whose dargah is found in the Mehrauli village.

RAIL MUSEUM

A hugely popular outing for children, the National Rail Museum offers a train ride which takes you around the museum filled with over 50 cars and engines from the mid 19th and 20th centuries. Most of these can be climbed on and explored. An indoor gallery has displays of traditional railway signals and lanterns, model trains and maps.

Location: Chanakyapuri. Tel. 011 2688 0804

RASHTRAPATI BHAVAN

Originally the palace of the Viceroy of India, Rashtrapati Bhavan is now the official residence of the President of India. It was designed by Sir Edward Lutyens, who was the chosen British architect for the city of New Delhi. Every Saturday there is a 'Change of the Guard' ceremony. From 16th February to 23rd March, visitors can explore the famous Mughal Garden with its nature trail and fruit-tree groves and book a tour of the house. The palace is built on Raisina Hill on the western end of Rajpath.

RED FORT (LAL QUILA)

The Red Fort was built with red sandstone and that's how it got its name. Emperor Shah Jahan built it in 1648 on the bank of the Yamuna River when he moved his imperial court from Agra to Delhi. The large walled fortress has pavilions, gardens and an audience room where the Emperor sat on the famous Peacock Throne. It once housed private pavilions, baths and gardens. A Sound and Light Show at dusk evokes the pageantry and splendour of Shah Jahan's reign.

REPUBLIC DAY PARADE

To celebrate becoming a sovereign and republic state, a spectacular parade is held each year on January 26th in Delhi that is best viewed along Rajpath at India Gate. The Army, Navy and Air-Force showcase their smartly attired marching regiments, followed by the Indian cavalry, NCC cadets, cultural programmes by schools and tableaus on floats representing most of India's 28 States and 7 Union territories. The Air Force fly-past features fighter planes performing special manoeuvres such as the 'Vertical Charlie'. The parade is very popular with children and it never fails to fill the hearts of Indians with national pride. Also taking part in the parade is a special contingent of children awarded for their bravery.

RICKSHAWS

Cycle rickshaws are found in certain neighbourhoods of NCR and Old Delhi and their numbers are increasing due to the demand for cheap transport across short distances. Some rickshawalas have their own vehicles but many of them hire from contractors, paying approx 25 rupees a day. It is a way of making a living without investment and new arrivals from villages who take up this work often have to sleep in the rickshaw at night. Some old-timers have picked up information from guides and get a good tip every now and then for enriching the ride with anecdotes.

Ss

SHAADI

Lively wedding scenes unfold on the streets especially from November through February when the weather is good. Look out for a baraat with a live band and the groom on a horse. Watch his friends and relatives dance on the streets as they approach the bride's house which is typically decorated with hundreds of fairy lights.

SLUMS

Half of Delhi's 15 million people live in slums. Rural folk from farming families unable to make ends meet in the villages tend to migrate to cities looking for work and can only afford rooms in slum areas which lack clean water, electricity and sanitation. Many of the city's household helpers, day labourers and vendors live here. To understand their lives, read the 'Delhi Green' NGO blog.

The Salaam Baalak Trust offers awareness walks.

Contact: salaamwalk@yahoo.com

SNAKE CHARMERS

As more and more people realise that snakes are endangered and belong in their natural habitat, Indian wildlife laws have banned the capture of snakes. Although snake charming is a dying profession, there remain, however, thousands of Saperas in India whose livelihood depends on this work and they are allowed to perform at specific tourist sites. Playing their haunting tune on a pungi or been, they rouse cobras, Russell's vipers, pythons or mangrove snakes from their baskets, Saperas are now being encouraged to focus on their music. *Palinath Snake Charmer performs outside the Rail Museum and can be contacted. Tel. 0129 6568628 OR 92 1122 1949*

SOUND AND LIGHT SHOWS

Delhi Tourism's spectacular Sound and Light shows can be experienced at the Old Fort and the Red Fort. At the new 'Ishq-e- Dilli' (The Spirit Of Delhi) show at the Old Fort, computer graphics, laser, audio-visual, light and sound effects complement the lively narration of the story of India from the 11th century to present day. The hour-long shows are in English and Hindi each evening. *For timings and tickets see DTTDC's website www.delhitourism.gov.in Tel. 91 11 4629 365*

STATE EMPORIA

A line-up of eighteen emporia on Baba Kharak Singh Marg represents the states of India. They are a treasure trove of the best textiles, crafts and decorative items from the states. Children can find some wonderful toys and gifts. *The more recently opened Kamla (the crafts shop) at 1, Rajiv Gandhi Handicrafts Bhavan, Baba Kharak Singh Marg has an updated and beautifully displayed selection of crafts and toys. Also explore Mother Earth at no 8, Tribes at no 2, and Hansiba at no 5.*

Tt

TANDOOR

A tandoor is a barrel-shaped earthen oven placed in or above the ground. It is wood or coal fired and cooks the food by exposing it to heat. Temperature in a tandoor often goes up to 480 degrees centigrade. Flat circles of dough are slapped and stuck on to its walls and crisp tandoori rotis are removed using long metal rods. Tandoors are also used for cooking meat and vegetables on skewers. They are often found in restaurants and neighbourhood dhabas.

TAXI

The distinctive black and yellow Ambassador taxis are an icon of Delhi. Called kaali-peeli by locals, they are fast becoming a relic with the arrival of radio taxis.

TOYS AND GAMES

Many traditional Indian toys, train-sets, tops, dolls and puppets are made of wood. Others are made from cotton and cloth, such as the colourful stuffed animals decorated with trim and woollen pom poms. Older children play cricket, badminton, football and hockey. The popular board games are ludo, snakes-and-ladders and chess, which originated in India in the 6th century. On the streets and neighbourhoods of Delhi, pitthu is played, where a team stacks up flat stone pieces into a tower and their opponents try and topple it with a ball. Flat pieces of marble were found discarded during the building boom, hence the natural evolution of this game. Stapu (hopscotch) where kids hop across squares marked on the ground is very popular too.

TRUCKS

Colourfully painted trucks are a delightful sight as they deliver goods all over Delhi. The truck owners take pride in their vehicles and have them decked out with paintings, tassels and hammered metal. Commonly seen motifs are the swan, lotus, peacock and the Indian flag. 'OK TATA' and 'HORN PLEASE' are usually painted on the rear, along with humorous phrases. The dangling black shoe is meant to ward off the evil eye.

Uu

UGRASEN KI BAOLI

This little known, ancient baoli or step-well is a hidden jewel on Hailey Road near Rajiv Chowk. The sunken stone structure, with niches and passageways, was built as a water reservoir and refuge from the summer's heat. Believed to be built by King Agrasen in the 14th century, it is now home to bats and pigeons.

UNIFORMS

Every morning and afternoon, groups of school children can be seen all over the city, making their way to school and back. You can also see them on school trips at places like the zoo, the monuments, museums and parks. Delhi has over 5000 schools and they generally fall under the following categories: Government, Local Body,

Private aided and Private unaided. There are also Kendria Vidyalayas (KVs) and Jawahar Navodya Vidyalayas (JNV). Several NGOs such as Pratham have established their own free baalwadis and teaching centres.

URINATORS

The sight of men urinating on walls and into open sewers is sadly a common one. As a large number of people walk from one area to another for work, they often do not have the time or do not know where to find the public urinals (which are usually based near neighbourhood markets). The Government needs to build many more toilets. Private organizations which aim to improve health and hygiene such as Sulabh International are much appreciated.

VENDORS

Street vending is the livelihood of many people who leave their rural homes for cities with a small amount of capital. They sell a variety of items such as fruits, vegetables, eggs, snacks, drinks, peanuts, toys, flowers, cigarettes, magazines. The people of the city get these items at reasonable prices and the vendors tend to be conveniently located. It is a hard life for vendors as it is not easy to get a legal permit to operate, they are hounded by the police and wholesale prices have gone up, making profits weaker. SEWA Delhi is trying to help vendors, especially women, to get licences and create hawker zones where they can vend legally with dignity.

VINTAGE CAR RALLY

Cars manufactured from 1919 to 1939 are classified as 'vintage' and the ones made from 1940 to 1956 are called 'classic.' Each year over a hundred cars participate in The Statesman Vintage Car Rally that starts at Statesman House in Rajiv Chowk. Prizes are awarded at the end of the run.

WARDING OFF THE EVIL EYE

Green chillies and lime are strung and hung outside shops and stalls, the black face of a repellent devil (nazar pattu) with his tongue sticking out hangs in front of homes and the colourful transport trucks have black shoes hanging off them. These are just some items used by people to ward off the evil eye.

WATER CART

The square, tin water carts can be seen all over Delhi. The top of the cart holds glasses, lemons and sometimes fresh mint. For 50 paisa, the vendor pumps a glassful of cold water, and for a rupee you can have a refreshing nimbu-pani or sweet lemonade. They quench the thirst of thousands of people especially in the summer.

WILDLIFE OF DELHI

After Nairobi, Delhi is known as the most bird-rich capital in the world with close to 450 species. Peafowl, kites and hawks can be spotted in local parks, gardens and forested areas. The Okhla Bird Sanctuary is particularly rewarding in the winter months when the migratory birds visit. Rhesus macaques, langurs, wild mongooses and snakes are to be found all over Delhi.

At the Asola Bhatti Wildlife Sanctuary, one can see many bird species and mammals like neelgai, rufus tailed hare, monitor lizard, Indian civet, common and small Indian mongoose. There are enclosures for blackbuck and cheetal. The Aravali Biodiversity Park is a 692 acre wilderness area protecting local flora and fauna.

WORDS ON VEHICLES

There isn't a dull moment on the roads of Delhi. People often come across transport trucks and auto-rickshaws which have humorous phrases, poetry and words of wisdom painted on the rear. One truck had a saying 'The rich live on biscuit and cake, the poor live on steering and brake' (translated from Hindi). An auto rickshaw had 'Even a dog does not bark without a reason'. This was clearly a rebuke to other drivers who tend to blow the horn unnecessarily. Delhiites love noting and sharing these phrases with each other.

X-CITING FESTIVALS

Through the year, Delhi has many exciting festivals. Children particularly enjoy smearing coloured powder on each other at Holi, lighting diyas and firecrackers during Diwali, watching Ram Leela and burning Ravan at Dussehra, celebrating Eid with gifts and opening presents and visiting Santa on Christmas.

YAMUNA

The Yamuna is one of India's major rivers with its source at Yamunotri in the Himalayas. It flows for 1370 kilometres through Delhi, Mathura and Agra before merging with the Ganga in Allahabad. It is sadly choked and polluted. Repairing the sewage system and cleaning the waters of the Yamuna is badly needed.

YELLOW PANSY BUTTERFLY

This exquisite butterfly is seen in Delhi gardens, often hovering over marigold flowers. It is mainly yellow with black and yellow spots on the forewings and apex and two large blue spots on each wing. It belongs to the Nymphalidae family. *A good place to spot this would be at the open air Butterfly Sanctuary in Lodhi Gardens or at the 'Butterfly Park' at the Garden of Five Senses near Qutab Minar.*

YOGA

Yoga is an ancient Indian spiritual and physical discipline. It is way of life that teaches us how to breathe deeply, gives us flexibility and channels our energy positively thereby optimising our abilities. In the gardens and parks of Delhi, yoga is practiced in the mornings, including laughter yoga.

Few noteworthy contacts for classes:

- Yogalife Studio in Defence colony, Tel. 98 1186 3332 www.yogalife.in

- Yoga Studio D-43 Hauz Khas. Seema Sondhi, Tel. 98 1113 1368

ZOO

Set against the magnificent backdrop of the Old Fort, the Delhi Zoo is where you can see Royal Bengal tigers, asiatic lions, indian rhinoceros, leopards and many other species from around the world. Many migratory birds visit each year. *Located on Mathura Road, Tel. 011 2435 9825.*

TO LEARN MORE

www.incredibleindia.org
www.delhitourism.nic.in
www.delhievents.com
www.delhiexplocity.com

Delightful Delhi

ALSO LOOK OUT FOR...

DANCES OF INDIA

Performances of Kathak, Bharatnatyam, Odissi, Bhangra, Garba and Naga dances can be seen at the popular Dances of India show where several styles can be experienced in a single hour long performance. *Location: Anjuman Hall, Bahadur Shah Zafar Marg, Tel. 2323 1228*

DELHI BY METRO - A GUIDED TOUR

This three to four hour tour is a delightful way of exploring Delhi via green transport modes like the metro, auto-rickshaws and cycle rickshaws. Enthusiastic students from the NGO Manzil start and end the tour at Rajiv Chowk, taking you to New and Old Delhi and stopping at popular eating places. *Contact: Deepa@delhimagic.com Tel.9867707414*

DEVI ARTS FOUNDATION

The Devi Arts Foundation, established by the Poddar family, provides a venue for contemporary artists from the subcontinent to engage and display their experimental works and the various creative thought processes prevalent today. Two shows a year are designed to familiarise children with trends in art and to help them engage with creative expressions. *Location: Sirpur House, Sector 44, Gurgaon, Tel. 0124 488817*

FORESTS OF DELHI

Hidden away from the traffic riddled roads, Delhi has a surprising amount of forested land with pathways for walks. Some of the noteworthy forests are the Ridge, Mehrauli Archeological Park, Jahanpanah City Forest and the Asola Wildlife reserve. *Free saplings are available from many nurseries under a Government scheme to make Delhi greener.*

HAUZ KHAS VILLAGE

The word 'Hauz Khas' refers to a royal tank built in this area which nestles in the beautiful surroundings of Deer park, with views of Feruz Shah's tomb, a seminary and the reservoir which has swans and ducks. The Hauz Khas Village complex has become a lively place to explore, shop, view art and eat. Heritage walks with INTACH can be booked to explore this area's history and architecture with an expert.

HOOKAH

The hookah is a smoking device where tobacco smoke is passed through a water chamber where it is purified and cooled. It is said to have originated in northwest India. A household item for many rural, agrarian families, the hookah is used as a form of relaxation and bonding with friends. You might see a man or a woman in the villages, slums or outskirts of Delhi sitting on a cot, enjoying a smoke. Trendy shisha bars in city clubs tend to have herbal substances rather than tobacco.

MUGHAL GARDENS

Each year in February and March, the most beautiful gardens in Delhi, Rashtrapati Bhavan's 320 acre Mughal Gardens come into bloom with colourful tulips, dahlias, chrysanthemums and several other flowers, herbs and trees. This is when they are open to the public. Landscaped and designed by Sir Edwin Lutyens, they are truly worth a visit, especially the Rose Garden and circular Butterfly Garden. *Check website for open days. Timings are from 9.30am to 2.30pm*

QUAINT SIGHTS

All you need to do is to have a keen eye and loads of quaint sights will leap out at you. In old Delhi, discover a bird hospital in a Jain temple, wedding garlands made of crisp hundred rupee notes and bags of chillies waiting to be traded in Khari Baoli. In sari shops moustachioed men regularly get up and model the saris on themselves. There are many miss-spelt words on billboards and a bizarre street sign which says, 'No elephants allowed here'. Foreigners find the sight of domestic animals such as chickens, pigs, goats and buffaloes wandering the streets quaint and endearing.

RAM LEELA PERFORMANCES

Children love the enactment of scenes from the Ramayana performed each year during the festival of Dussehra at the Ramleela Grounds, Red Fort, Bhartiya Kala Kendra and other venues. Although performances begin on the festival of Navratri and continue over eleven days, the best day to watch is the tenth, when effigies of Ravan and his brothers are burned.

RUINS EVERYWHERE

Delhi is a very historic City filled with archaeological sites comparable to Rome and Athens. It is known to have been the capital of several ancient empires. Old Fort is believed to be the site for Indraprastha, the capital of the Pandavas mentioned in the Mahabharatha from 5000 BC. Since then, King Ashoka, Prithviraj Chauhan, the Tughlak Dynasty, the Sultanate, the Moghuls and the

British built cities here. By just keeping an eye open one can appreciate the layers of history. While walking, driving, picnicking or playing cricket, you may well have enjoyed a stunningly beautiful and historic backdrop.

SANSKRITI KENDRA

One of Delhi's hidden jewels, this atmospheric complex has three museums showcasing everyday art, tribal art and textiles. Enjoy the beautiful grounds as you explore Madhubani murals, terracotta figures and Warli paintings. They also have a library, amphitheatre and art gallery. An Artists in Residence programme encourages the sharing of traditional skills and development of new ideas. *Location: Mehrauli Gurgaon Road. Look out for Anandgram in Aya Nagar, Tel.9111 26501796*

SAULABH INTERNATIONAL TOILET MUSEUM

Although it is an unusual subject for a museum collection, the toilet museum experience is an educational and interesting one. In the spotlessly clean atmosphere, learn about the history of toilet systems and customs related to the business of going to the toilet. Away from the museum, the very welcome Sulabh Movement provides and maintains toilets in many areas in India where there were no toilets *Location: Palam Dabri Marg, New Delhi, Tel.25031518*

UNRULY TRAFFIC

Delhi's roads are crowded with buses, trucks, cars, auto rickshaws, two wheelers, rickshaws, bicycles, carts pulled by animals and pedestrians. Drivers jostle for position, cut across lanes, use the outer lanes to overtake and go through red lights. The horn is regularly blown as a warning to others. The roads are, however, lively with colourful trucks, funny words behind vehicles and interesting people.

WALKS

- Exploring Delhi's narrow alleyways, bazaars and green areas can be vey rewarding. The India Habitat Centre organizes Heritage, Historic and Nature Walks with specialist guides. *Contact: www.habitatworld.com/events-walks*
Tel. 011 4366 3080

- The Indian National Trust for Art and Cultural Heritage (INTACH) offers guided walks to places such as the Mehrauli Archeologicsl Park, Chandini Chowk, Hauz Khas and Lodi Gardens. *Location: 71, Lodhi Estate*

Surekha Narain runs a business with 2 hour long customised private walks.
Contact: surekhan@hotmail.com Tel. 9811330098

Delightful Delhi
SPOTTING GAME

1. Can you spot the Athpula Bridge with eight arches in Lodhi Gardens?

2. Find a funny phrase behind a truck or a three-wheeler scooter

3. Look for King Chandragupta's famous Iron Pillar near Qutab Minar.

4. Can you spot a newly-wed lady wearing a choora of red and white bangles on both wrists?

5. Many people hang a painted clay nazar pattu or devil's face on the front of their home to ward off the evil eye. Can you find one?

6. Spot a stray cow or a dog on the streets of Delhi.

7. Can you find the elephant skull at the Railway Museum? This elephant crashed into a train once.

8. Spot a peacock, a myna or a monkey in Delhi's green areas.

9. Look for a rare White Tiger of Rewa in the Delhi Zoo.

10. Can you spot lemon and green chillies strung in Delhi's shops, vending carts and homes?

ABOUT THE AUTHOR

Geetika Jain is a travel writer and the author of several children's picture books. With this travel book on Delhi she hopes that young readers will further appreciate this endearing city.

ABOUT THE PHOTOGRAPHER

Arjun Jain is currently studying at Princeton University and he finds rich material for photographs in every turn and corner of Delhi.